Is It God's Good Plan to Crush and Grieve You?

Is It God's Good Plan to Crush and Grieve You?

A New/Old Model of Marriage Restoration

D. E. FAST

RESOURCE *Publications* · Eugene, Oregon

IS IT GOD'S GOOD PLAN TO CRUSH AND GRIEVE YOU?
A New/Old Model of Marriage Restoration

Resource Publications
An Imprint of Wipf and Stock Publishers
199 W. 8th Ave., Suite 3
Eugene, OR 97401

www.wipfandstock.com

PAPERBACK ISBN: 979-8-3852-1214-9
HARDCOVER ISBN: 979-8-3852-1215-6
EBOOK ISBN: 979-8-3852-1216-3

04/19/24

This book is dedicated to my son, Sammy:
You are bravest, most loving, persistent, and beautiful young
man I know. You are Mom's and my gift from God. We both
love you dearly, Bud!

"All praise to God, the Father of our Lord Jesus Christ. God is our merciful Father and the source of all comfort. He comforts us in all our troubles so that we can comfort others. When they are troubled, we will be able to give them the same comfort God has given us."
2 Cor 1:3–4

Contents

Contents

Preface

I COULDN'T FIX IT. Even after twenty years and some serious detours, I was still struggling in my marriage. I knew, deep down I loved my wife, but we were so different in so many ways. It seemed like everything I tried made things worse, not better.

Then God brought Eph 5 into my life. I knew from reading the Bible, that this chapter was supposed to be the one that would give me what I needed. But it seemed the more I read what Paul (the author) presented, the more confused I got and the more questions I had. The most persistent was, "How do I love my wife in the same way Jesus loved His church?" This book was written to answer that question.

.

Introduction

LIVING IN A DIFFICULT or dying marriage hurts. Thoughts of divorce make it worse. The daily pain and confusion of trying to figure out what to do becomes overwhelming. After a time, thoughts of drinking, using, secretly hooking up, or even ending our life seem like better options.

And then there's the added pain of suffering alone. We get the idea that if we say it out loud, or ask for help, it's an admission, that things really are as bad as they are. It becomes easier to focus on her faults and to blame, instead of taking responsibility for the harsh and hurtful things we've said and done. Loss of hope creeps in, along with unwanted thoughts of no longer wanting to live.

I just described a little of what I went through before and after I got divorced. You may be in the middle of experiencing something like what I just shared. If so, I'm sorry. But there's hope! This is the reason for the opening verse. God is our merciful Father and the source of our comfort. He will comfort us in our troubles by bringing someone along who's been where we're at, to help comfort us with the same comfort God gave them.

God restoring my marriage was one of the greatest miracles He's ever done for me. What I thought was impossible, He made possible. I'm hoping I can come along side and share with you some of the insights God gave me while He was restoring my marriage. My hope is that after reading this book, He will give you the hope, encouragement, and insights you need to keep going in your efforts to either improve or restore your marriage.

The Behind the Words Story

As you're going to see, I'll be speaking from personal experience. I'm going to do my best to be real and vulnerable about my mistakes, sins, poor character, and losses. But also, I want to share about the God who graciously and lovingly stepped in and restored what I lost, my marriage.

It's important to me that you get a real picture of who I am as the author. I found, that when I was going through the pain of divorce, I didn't want to listen to people who told me how life and marriage was supposed to be. I wanted to listen to those who had actually gone through the hell I was going through and were willing to share the humiliating details that exposed their sins and mistakes. The more real they were, the more I trusted them. I found hope and insight from people who took responsibility for their faults in the divorce, not those who were still stuck in shame and blame. The more broken they were, the more help I got for what I had broken.

With that out of the way, I'd like to start sharing my story from just after I graduated Bible college: I was hired by the college as a traveling speaker/recruiter for several years. I then worked full-time as a youth pastor and in youth-type ministries for around fifteen.

My wife, Laurie, and I started dating almost immediately after I left my last youth position. We were married about a year and a half after that, and I went back to school. During this time our son, Sammy, was born.

Almost immediately after Sammy was released from the hospital, we headed off to serve as head pastor in a small church. For the past twenty or so years I've been counseling folks struggling with illegal substance use in outpatient and residential settings.

It's important that I give you a bit more information about Sammy's birth and some of the challenges that went along with it. He was born three and a half months early. He was diagnosed with significant cerebral palsy and chronic lung disease. He has never walked or talked. He breathes through a machine 24/7 and eats through a tube in his stomach. He has been our beautiful, perfect gift from God for over twenty-five years.

Both Laurie and I were shattered, confused and heartbroken when the doctors gave Sammy's diagnosis. We had lots of activities, hopes, and dreams for him that now had to be reworked.

I remember sitting at a dining room table at the Ronald McDonald house with Laurie, both of us silent, not knowing what to say, tears in our eyes, and trying to make sense of the news we'd just heard. I was having a hard time trying to figure out how my loving God could do something like this to our precious son.

I didn't know it then, but I believe it was at this time that my faith and trust in God began to weaken. I started to believe that God wasn't good and didn't have a good plan for us that was full of "future and hope" (Jer 29:11). I got stuck in anxiety, fear, and depression. I began to expect the worst from God.

Besides the heartbreak and confusion that went along with Sammy's condition, there were huge medical bills from his extended stay (over three months) in specialized care. We had no insurance, and I was overwhelmed. We then moved quite a distance (away from caring family and friends) to begin the new ministry. We also purchased an older home that required a lot of time and hard work to remodel. And there was still my new wife and marriage I was trying to figure out.

I allowed Sammy's challenges to have a negative impact on my marriage. The Laurie I was getting to know, and try to love, wasn't the same Laurie I'd dated. I didn't know it then, but I changed as well. Something in me broke. I began to hate God and mistreat Laurie.

It was during this time that I began to take my fears, life-pressures, and confusions out on Laurie. I was rude, disrespectful, and said horrible things to her in anger. I was relationally, maritally, and emotionally out of control. Laurie finally got tired of who I had become and how I was treating her and filed for divorce (this was my fault, not hers).

We were divorced for seven years. It took that long for God to humble and change me so that I could begin to trust and love Him a bit more, realize and remember that He is always good, and begin to believe there was a chance Laurie and I could get back together. It also took this long for God to show Laurie that He had been doing some work in me and for her to be able to trust me again. By God's kindness and grace, He made it possible for us to start dating and eventually get remarried. We have been together for over fifteen years now.

It's important to me that you know my failings and sins as you read. Shared weaknesses make friends. Shared successes make heroes. My time in substance counseling taught me that when someone is really hurting, having someone whose fallen into the same hole they're in (friend) and found a way out is far more helpful than someone whose never been there or is so unsure of God's grace, they can't admit their failures (hero).

Target Audience

THIS BOOK IS WRITTEN to Christian men who are struggling in or have lost their marriage. If this is where you're at, I'm sorry. The year before and the first five years of my divorce were the worst of my life. While I was going through it, I lost my desire to live.

I couldn't afford a counselor. The closest thing I could think of was to start going to Alcohol Anonymous groups. After two years or so of AA, I began going to Saturday morning Al-Anon meetings. These were geared more to family members who had loved ones with various addictions. I will forever be grateful for the people there, who took me in, accepted me, and came alongside me in my time of confusion and hopelessness.

I found so much healing and comfort during this time. I'm not really sure I can remember much of what was said. What I can remember is leaving the meeting with a sense of lightness and relief; that I wasn't the only one; that I wasn't alone; and there were others who were going through very similar losses, and feeling hopeless, just like me.

Not only did I receive weekly insight and relief for my pain, but God then used what He allowed me to go through, to be able to relate to and come alongside others who weren't just struggling with substances, but the many times even greater pains of relational loss and regret. I would never ask to go through what I went through during my divorce. But looking back at all the lives and families God touched through my weaknesses and failures makes having gone through it easily worth it.

So again, if you're struggling in, or have lost your marriage, you're not alone. There's a whole bunch of us out here who either have or are going through something pretty close to what you're going through. My hope is that, God will give you the grace to continue to "patiently endure the same things we *have or are suffering*."[1]

---

1. Author's paraphrase of 2 Cor 1:6b–7.

Before I Tell You What I'm Going to Tell You

I HAVE A FEAR that if we don't cover some initial insights (before you hear this method), it'll be too difficult to handle, and I'll lose some of you. One of the things that comes along with intense, God-directed pain is a real sense of weakness and a sincere realization of how desperately we need Him, an internal desperation that says, "If You don't do this it's not going to get done" or "If You don't step in and get me through this, I'm never going to make it."

This may be hard to hear, but this desperation is actually a really good thing and exactly where we need to be in order for us to cry out to God and ask for His help, instead of the useless belief that we can somehow do this on our own.

What I'm talking about is asking for the same angel God sent Jesus to strengthen Him, and ask for God to give us the same help (Luke 22:43) or to desperately cry out and choose to trust (many times in spite of untrusting emotions) for God's new, eagle's-wing power (Is 40:31), or, even if we're not exactly sure how, to intensely ask Jesus to live His Gal 2:20 life through us and to realize that in order for us to follow through with what's going to be presented here, we'll need to be utterly dependent on the Holy Spirit's power, not our own (Zech 4:6). Having a sense of desperation, inadequacy, and being at the end of our ropes will be exactly where God wants us to be as we move forward.

Getting humbled, surrendering, and asking for help isn't something that comes natural to most of us. We want (for the most part) to believe we can do it on our own. Handouts aren't something that sits well with us. But if you want to call it that, we're all going to need a handout from God on this one. This is one of those things that we will never be able to do on our own. It most likely is going to take some scratching, clawing, and possibly cussing on our part for God to get us where we need to be. And that being our gut-level admission of "I can't do this." The biblical truth is "if God doesn't *rebuild our marriages, the only thing we're going to build is shacks. If God doesn't get our wives and marriages back, we might* as well take a nap."[1]

For the first few years of our divorce, it seemed like the harder I tried, the worse it got. Most of my efforts ended up with Laurie crying and me heading back to my place, confused and hopeless. But for quite some time, and even as recently as this week, Laurie and I have seen God make things work for us that could never have happened unless He was the One doing it. One of the primary reasons for this is because God finally got His way with me and got me out of the way.

This is what it's going to take in order to get our wives and marriages back. He's got this! This whole process will go so much better if we let Him have it. And at the same time, it'll be okay if you continue to try to do it on your own. He will continue to work with you to get you to the place He wants you to be, completely dependent on Him.

I am going to work really hard during this process to not make any promises. I think that would be cruel and dishonest. I don't know what God has for you, your wife, or your marriage. I can't guarantee that what God did for me and Laurie is going to happen for you. But what I can say is that what's going to be presented here is straight from the Bible. And if it worked for Jesus, and Jesus through Paul is telling us to do it, there's at least a fair reason to "dare to hope" (Lam 3:21).

---

1. Author's paraphrase of Ps 127:1 (MSG).

We're Going to Want to Do This

THERE'S THIS HEARTBREAKING STORY in Luke 7 where Jesus is comparing a New Testament pastor-type (Pharisee) with a woman who in verse 37 is identified as being "immoral." The reason I'm sharing this story is because there may come a time (and you may already be in it) where you aren't seeing your wife as anything other than a broken or "immoral" person. The goal of this section is to get us to see her from Jesus' eyes, not the Pharisees'.

In the story, Simon was critical, judgmental, and unforgiving, because he believed he was better than the obviously flawed woman in front of him. He was stuck in the truth of who she *was,* not who she had b*ecome*: fully forgiven, unconditionally loved, free from her past, and grateful because of what Jesus had done for her (verses 36–50).

Another reason I'm introducing this story is because I'm hoping you won't be like me and hang onto previous failings of your wife. It's going to be difficult to graciously love and disciple her (as we're going to see later), if we see ourselves as having specks in our eyes and only logs in her's (Matt 7:3–5).

My mistake was to define Laurie based on her imperfections, instead of seeing her from God's perspective of being pure and holy and without fault (Col 1:22). It was tough to love and accept her when I was stuck in resentments. I focused on how I'd been hurt, instead of how I'd been hurting her.

This story is a story of me and Laurie—and possibly you and your wife. It hurts every time I read it. It hurts to be a Simon. It hurts even more to be around one. Resentments, fault-finding, and

8

projecting unacceptance sucks the life out of our wives. Receiving constant reminders of what they've done and who they were drains our wives' hope of ever being seen as anything other than an "immoral" woman.

We can believe we're better than we are if we keep our eyes on her faults instead of our own. But just the fact that we're focusing on her faults and not forgiving her is a sin we'll need to repent and ask forgiveness for. "Who are you to condemn *your wife*?"[1] Proverbs 14:11 says, "Smart people know how to hold their tongue; their grandeur is to forgive and forget" (MSG).

The people we love most are the ones who could have pointed out our faults and sins, but instead overlooked them and showed grace and forgiveness. If we're going to be restoring our marriages, one of the first places we're going to want to start is to drop the stones and throw forgiveness instead. This is, like we looked at earlier, impossible without Him doing it through us. It is however one of the ways (as we're going to see later) that we'll have to ask God to give us the ability to forgive, love, and serve our wives, even if at first we don't believe she deserves it.

It would be far better for our wives and marriages if we could authentically say, "I know who you are." But instead of focusing on her past, we remind her of who she really is: forgiven, loved, and accepted by us, just like the woman in this story.

---

1. Author's paraphrase of verse 11.

We Place Too Much Faith in Our Feelings

People in pain make poor choices. Depending on how long and how bad the pain has been in our marriages, we tend to focus on it, instead of the good God is accomplishing through it.

Pain screams; the Holy Spirit whispers. His reminders that He's always living inside us usually come in a whisper (1 Kgs 19:11–13; Rom 8:9). What He's whispering through our pain is that He's there with us in the middle of it (Mark 4:35–41); that He's making all things new (Rev 21:5); that He's working through our pain for our good (Rom 8:28); and that He cares deeply about the pain that we and our wives are going through right now. Matthew 10:29–31 says, "What's the price of a pet canary? Some loose change, right? And God cares what happens to it even more than you do. He pays even greater attention to you, down to the last detail—even numbering the hairs on your head! So don't *fear that you're alone and that He doesn't care.* You're worth more than a million canaries."[1]

We're going to want to ask God to give us the grace to trust Him (His love, caring, and compassion for us and our wives) more than the pain we're feeling in our marriages.

---

1. Author's paraphrase from the MSG.

Experiential Trainings

ONE OF THE WAYS God has of helping us become more like Him and the husbands we need to be is through the use of experiential trainings. The Bible uses words and phrases such as sifting, pruning, the discipline of the Lord, trials, and problems (Luke 22:31; John 15:1–17; Heb 12:5–6; Jas 1:2–4; Rom 5:3–5) to describe experiential trainings.

God uses the Bible in our lives to change us (2 Tim 3:16; Heb 4:12). To reinforce, solidify, and make real what He's showing us in it is to put us through experiential trainings.

The problem for many of us is that we're more concerned about getting out from underneath these trainings than we are in learning and growing from them. In the context of what we're talking about here, these experiential trainings are going to come through our difficult marriages.

What I'm going to say next is going to be hard to hear, especially when you're most likely in the middle of extreme suffering: the marital pain you're experiencing is far less important than learning and growing from it.

James 1:2–4 says, "Dear brothers and sisters, when troubles of any kind come your way, consider it an opportunity for great joy. For you know that when your faith is tested, your endurance has a chance to grow. So let it grow, for when your endurance is fully developed, you will be perfect and complete, needing nothing."

Hebrews 12:2 says, "Because of the joy awaiting him, he endured the cross." The joy awaiting Jesus was the applause He was going to get from God for having completed God's good plan of crushing and grieving Him (Isa 53:10–12).

Another motivation for Jesus to continue to endure extreme suffering was to stay intimately connected to God's love. He did this through His obedience to His Father. John 15:9–10 says, "I have loved you even as the Father has loved me. Remain in my love. When you obey my commandments, you remain in my love, just as I obey my Father's commandments and remain in his love."

In the context of the pain and sufferings we're currently going through, we'll want to ask God to give us the ability to be obedient and be more passionate about following through with His experiential trainings than we are about getting out from underneath them.

Soaring Instead of Stumbling

THIS THOUGHT TIES IN with the last section. Isaiah 40:31 says, "But those who trust in the Lord will find new strength. They will soar high on wings like eagles. They will run and not grow weary. They will walk and not faint." In the middle of our marital pains (experiential trainings), many times we faint. Our fainting takes the form of anger, frustration, blaming, giving up, or infidelities. To stay in the marital process of change, we're going to want to trust Him and His experiential trainings, not books, techniques, or ourselves.

One of the problems with so many of the books (and the techniques they promote) is that there's something in us that thinks, "Because this source (including the Bible) tells me I should do something, this must mean I have the ability to do it." Here's where we get into all kinds of problems.

The Bible has many directives (things God tells us to do). We could call these laws, or things we're supposed to obey. But just because God and the Bible tell us to do something, doesn't mean *we* have the ability to do it. Jesus said in John 15:5, "For apart from me you can do nothing." Or Paul telling us in Phil 4:13 that he could "do all things through Him who strengthens me." It's in our trusting in what He has and will do for us that gives us the ability to soar on His eagle's-wing power.

An example of one of these laws is when Paul in Eph 5:25 tells us to love our wives in the same way Jesus loved the church. We'd think that because we've been told to do it, we must therefore have the ability. But, as you may have already found out, you can't—and neither could I. We don't have what it takes (on our own).

On the other hand, anytime the Bible exposes what God has, is, or will do for us, it's called grace. Grace is the opposite of law. The law tells us what to do but doesn't give us the ability to do it. Grace on the other hand, is God doing for us, what He's told us to do.

Jesus said in John 3:3 that we have to be "born again" or saved. We can't do this. But, God by His grace does it for us. Ephesians 2:8 says, "God saved you by his grace when you believed. And you can't take credit for this; it is a gift from God." That's grace. And we're going to need it to keep from stumbling and keep going with what (as we're going to see later), God is calling us to do in Eph 5 and Isa 53.

Stumbling in our efforts to restore our marriages is going to happen. But the stumbling is going to happen far less frequently as we trust God for His promised, new-eagle's-wing strength.

Before We Say "I Do"

THIS SECTION IS GOING to take some flexibility and open-mindedness on your part. It's going to seem fairly useless, because your decision to marry took place years ago. But because many men reading this book are most likely struggling in their marriage, it might bring some helpful understanding as to what you're currently going through.

I'm going to believe that the insights and information Laurie and I got during our premarriage counseling sessions was probably close to what every other Christian couple got or is getting in America today.

Both Laurie and I loved and respected the counselor who met with us. He was a good guy, with a big heart, who knew and loved both of us. The sad part was, what we got during those sessions was pretty anemic when it came to preparing us for what we were going to need in marriage. What he shared with us was most likely from a generic, Christian counseling manual, instead of the hard to hear, biblical truths that are going to be presented in this section.

Premarriage counseling needs to be less about, "Wherever you go, I will go; wherever you live, I will live" (Ruth 1:16–17), and more about the problems we're going to go through, where they're coming from, and how to address them.

Premarriage counseling needs to tell the couple what their biblical roles and responsibilities will be to each other. Not only that, but they'll also need to be told that whether they're prepared for it or not. Genesis 3 (as we're going to see later) is going to have a huge impact on their marriage. I know what I'm going to present next is going to sound pretty pessimistic, but better to have the spare tire and not need it, than to need it and not have it. The reality is that every Christian couple is going to need this spare.

In addition to whatever premarital information the counselor has been giving, what God pronounced would happen to the first couple (an ultimately every future couple) needs to be added. Somewhere in however many sessions the couple receives, they're going to need to hear something that resembles this:

1. I'm going to ask the two of you to first read separately and then, together, talk through how you see 1 Cor 7 applying to your marriage.

2. Glorifying God in your marriage is more important than either of you receiving your primary relational satisfaction from it: "*Marriage's* chief end is to glorify God, and to enjoy Him forever."[1]

3. God gets glorified when the two of you get along and accept each other (Rom 12:16a; 15:7), far more than the two of you being comfortable, completely compatible, or fulfillingly intimate.

4. As the future husband, you need to know there's going to be spiritual flaws in your wife. You don't see them now, but you will eventually. It's going to be your responsibility to disciple and help her work through them (Eph 5:21–23).

5. As the husband, there's a high likelihood you're going to either rule harshly, sinfully dominate, or drop your Eph 5 headship responsibilities.

6. How you relate to your future wife will be based on:

    a. Where you're at in your relationship with Jesus.

    b. Where you're at in your broken humbleness towards God (Matt 5:3).

    c. How consistently you're allowing Jesus to live His life through you (Gal 2:20).

1. Author's paraphrase of the Westminster Shorter Catechism.

d. How much you understand and are prepared to deal with the Gen 3 curse in your marriage.

e. How much you understand your role of headship that God has commissioned you to (Eph 5:22–24).

7. You're going to want to find an older, wiser, and longtime married Christian husband or widower who is or was married for at least twenty years, to help you figure out how to lovingly and graciously disciple your wife, and work through the challenges brought on by the curse.

8. As the wife, there's a high likelihood you're going to either have a tendency to attempt to rule, control, dominate, subvert, disrespect, or manipulate your husband. These behaviors are going to cause huge problems in your marriage. Unless you understand the marital repercussions of Gen 3, you won't know why, or where they're coming from. You're going to want to study and understand how the curse is going to influence you and negatively impact your marriage.

9. You're also going to want to talk to an older, wiser, longtime married Christian wife or widower who is or was married for at least twenty years. Your priority will be, as a means of glorifying God, learn to biblically respect and submit to your husband. Also, if you're not already doing it, work on developing trustworthiness, honesty, and a good work ethic (Prov 31:10–31; 1 Pet 3:3–6; Eph 5:22, 33).

10. Both of you will want to ask God to give you a passion and resolve to stay married (Mark 10:9).

11. Because you're both feeling so in love right now, you may believe that what you're hearing only applies to other couples (because your love is special and unique). Your love for each other is unique. But not so unique that it will keep you from having to work through the effects of the curse in your marriage.

The purpose of this section is to point out that, along with whatever information you may have gotten in your premarriage sessions, being exposed to Gen 3, and Eph 5, would have given priceless information as to why you're going through what you may be going through now. You'd still have problems. But the added information would have shown where the problems came from and how to work through them. It would've been far better to potentially be offended or possibly confused about whether or not to go through with the marriage, than to go into marriage unprepared.

If after reading this section you're telling yourself that some of this information is new and would have been helpful to hear before you got married, it's going to be okay. No matter who did your counseling, or what you did or didn't hear, God's still in charge and He wanted the two of you together, in spite your difficulties. And His timing and plans are perfect. The good news is, you're going to get to hear it now.

A Damnable Phrase

I T ' S S A D T O S E E how many unbiblical ideas, techniques, practices, principles, and sayings sneak into Christian marriages from the non-Christian world. One of these unbiblical thoughts is "happy wife—happy life." This many-times repeated quote is little more than a reinforcement of the Gen 3 curse passed into our marriages. There will be times when our wives, due to our fulfilling our God-given headship role, will not be happy. If we were to make her happy in those instances, we would be sinning.

I'm not saying we shouldn't attempt to please or make our wives happy. But if we make a higher priority of pleasing her instead of Him, we will have compromised our love for Him and our biblical responsibilities. As Christian husbands, our greatest joy and happiness comes from pleasing God, not our wives. Jesus said that His energy came from obeying His Father (John 4:34). This will be true of us as well. God will be pleased (possibly not our wives) as we (in His power) fulfill our role as head for our wives, and evidence this through our practiced priority of loving Him more than her (Eph 5:23; Luke 14:26). The primary way we show Jesus that we love Him is through our obedience. John 14:21 says, "The one who obeys me is the one who loves me" (TLB).

We'll want to ask God to give us a passion to first make Him happy by demonstrating our love for Him through our obedience. And then, as we continue to obey Him—her.

Breaking the Marriage No-Talk Rule

THE MARRIAGE NO-TALK RULE (MNTR) is fairly easy to identify (as long as it's in someone else's marriage). When it's in ours, it's a lot more complicated. It's complicated because for the most part we've never heard of it, and it's so widely (and unknowingly) practiced in marriage. When it's in place, we'll have many negative thoughts and emotions, but won't be able to identify where they're coming from.

From the husband's perspective it looks something like this: I say, ask, or do something that hurts, upsets, angers, or saddens my wife. Because I don't like it when she cries, gets silent, leaves the room, gets angry, tells me to sleep on the couch or stay at my folk's house for the night, I, as the wanna-keep-the-peace husband, learn fairly quickly that if I want to keep any of these repercussions from happening, it's better to keep my mouth shut, and not say, ask, or do anything that upsets her (refer back to "happy wife—happy life").

Some or many of the things we say, ask, or do, need to be said, asked or done. But if the MNTR is in place, we won't do them. If this is the case, we have effectively resigned our role of headship and have made a higher priority of pleasing our wives instead of God. The MNTR is now working and negatively affecting our marriages. It's doing what it does by keeping silent and hidden what needs to be exposed.

Another thing about the MNTR is that it's usually unspoken. What I mean by this is the MNTR gets put in place subliminally, by quietly sneaking in, under our relational radar. There are usually no discussions identifying it or contracts signed committing the two of us not to use it.

An example of this might be as the two of us are reading the Bible together and come across "wives, submit to your husbands, as is fitting for those who belong to the Lord. Husbands, love your wives and never treat them harshly" (Col 3:19–20). These two verses speak directly to the two main marital problems (as we're going to see later) inherited from the curse. But instead of talking through them (believing it could cause problems) we stay quiet and let it go.

The MNTR is usually established through marital cause and effect. We did this and that happened. Since we didn't like what happened, we keep quiet in hopes it won't happen again. Eventually we get frustrated with the dysfunctional silence and start to believe we either married the wrong person, that there's no hope for the marriage, or choose to live in an unhealthy, dissatisfying coexistence. Overall, we fear marital distancing and discord, so we keep quiet.

But here's the problem: there are many times what we say, ask, or do is not wrong, ignorant, selfish, or sinful. It's just something that needs to be said, asked, or done. Nothing sinful, just necessary. Instead of doing what we should, we cower and give into the rule and sacrifice long-term marital growth and potential intimacy for short-term marital peace.

Besides saying yes to our wives when we should have said no, and saying no to God when we should have said yes, we'll miss out on potential opportunities for improved trust, shared vulnerabilities, acceptance of each other's weaknesses, and furthered intimacy.

At the very least, it creates relational distance due to the inability to trust one another with what we believe, think, or feel. Initially, what gave a sense of peace and safety, eventually rewards us with relational loneliness.

The no-talk rule is brutal on marriages. An example would be when one of us gets annoyed (relational molehill) and, instead of humbly talking through it, we keep quiet and allow it to turn into a relational mountain that, if unchecked, evolves into an irreconcilable difference and possibly divorce. It's the power of the MNRT, not major differences that ends many marriages.

We're going to want to ask God to help us identify when the MNTR is taking place and for Him to give us the ability to kindly and graciously say it out loud.

The Thing Every Husband
Doesn't Want to Do

ON OUR WEDDING DAY, we don't know what we don't know. What we believe we know is that the beautiful woman coming down the aisle is the love of our life, the one we've waited our entire lives for. In our minds, she's perfect.

Most of us don't go into marriage telling ourselves that the one we've chosen looks like she'll bring a pretty good return on investment. Or that she's a darn good DIY fixer-upper project. We didn't mentally size her up as having good bones and in need of just a little TLC. We didn't walk around during our engagement telling friends and family that we were looking forward to doing, from the ground up, a complete nuts-and-bolts restoration on our fiancées. None of these thoughts or actions are built into our marital DNA. We didn't get married to work on our wives in the same way we look forward to working on our trucks, bikes, or boats.

None of these thoughts or ideas were floating around my head on the day of my marriage. What I was thinking was that I was the luckiest guy in the world and that Laurie and her family were perfect. I was convinced I was the one who needed fixing, not her. I had no clue of what was being asked of me in Eph 5. I never took it or Gen 3 seriously. For the most part, I never thought either of these passages applied to me.

I'm going to believe based on what I've read and the many dating and marriage counseling sessions I've given, I'm not the only one. It seems the majority of Christian men in America have the same mindset I had when it came to understanding and applying these two passages; we're sure they're important (because they're in the Bible), but not what we got married for.

It's common to accept the faulty messages being given through songs, movies, books, social media, parents, and sadly churches. They tell us that once the ring is on her finger, the emptiness in our hearts will be filled and our long-time loneliness will be taken care of. But hearing songs and seeing movies promoting our responsibility to suffer, serve, and sacrifice for the sake of our wives' spiritual growth, and health of our marriages, aren't anywhere to be found.

I know what I'm going to be presenting, about the Eph 5 work that needs to take place, is not what we got married for. But, if we're going to be obedient and take seriously what Jesus is telling us, we're going to want to ask God to give us the desire to have this be what we deep down inside want to do.

What's in Your Tent?

THERE'S A COUPLE OF convicting passages that ask the same question in the Old Testament book of Amos and are repeated in the New Testament book of Acts. "Was it to me you were bringing sacrifices and offerings during the forty years in the wilderness, Israel? No, you served your pagan gods—Sakkuth your king god and Kaiwan your star god—the images you made for yourselves" (Amos 5:25–26; Acts 7:42–43).

God is making a statement in the form of a question through Amos and Stephen. Obviously He knew what was going on. He just wanted them to know that He knew.

We no longer live in tents and aren't carving wooden or stone images. But is there a possibility that God might be using these two passages to expose to us that part of the problems we're having in our marriages is because we've been secretly worshiping "the ground she walks on" instead of Him?

If someone would have asked me ten years ago if I'd made an idol of Laurie, I would have first thought it was a weird question. Next, I would have said "no." But today (or say five years ago), I'd have to say "yes."

The last five years of my life have been really painful. God has been exposing and taking away the thing I worshiped more than anything else: the hope of having an intimate, love-filled relationship with my future wife. I unknowingly had been worshiping the idol I made of marriage and my fantasies surrounding it, behind the walls of my mental and emotional tent. God used this passage in Acts to expose to me, that I had secretly made a higher priority of love and marriage than my love for Him. What I mean by secretly is that it was secret even to me.

One of the reasons God brings and allows struggles in our marriages is to expose that we may have done this same thing. If we have, we'll end up trying to get from her what only He can give. We'll place unrealistic expectations on our wives, to meet the love and intimacy needs that only He is capable of meeting.

Because of these unachievable expectations, we'll end up resenting her for not fulfilling our long-held desires and fantasies. We'll place on her (either spoken or not) a demand that says she needs to be for us what only God can be, God.

These problems are due to false worship, not her inability to be a good wife. We're going to create struggles in our marriage, from these idolatries and we won't even know how they got there without God exposing this sin.

Another problem that arises is that it's going to be tough to follow through on what God is telling us to do in Eph 5. We won't risk upsetting her because like every other god, they need to be appeased, not angered. We'll end up falling back into the MNTR or the "happy wife—happy life" syndrome in order to keep the peace and continue to get whatever we were hoping to get from our misguided peace offerings.

If any of this applies, we're going to want to confess it as sin and ask God to take our marital idols away. God loves us so much that He doesn't want us to miss out on what we could be receiving from Him, during our times of secret worship, of Him, instead of her, in our tents.

The Number One Cause
of Marital Problems

FOR THE LONGEST TIME, I read highly recommended marital and relational books that I then asked (or politely demanded) Laurie read as well. We tried working through manuals that some of our friends used. It took energy, time, and money to try these helps. But when they failed to work, it made me (and I'm pretty sure Laurie) feel like our marriage was more broken than we thought.

These books and manuals seemed to focus on techniques such as improving communication, learning love languages, that better sex starts in the kitchen, and that somehow our parents were the ones to blame for our problems. For the most part, nothing we used helped. None of the resources we tried ever dealt with our two main problems: my anger and harshness, and her control and disrespect.

It wasn't until God showed us that the answers for our two persistent problems was in Gen 3. In this chapter, God pronounces a curse on Adam and Eve because of their disobedience. The sad truth is that many non-Christians don't know, and many Christians seem to ignore it. But what we don't know or choose to ignore can hurt us; and in this case, be the cause of many of our "irreconcilable differences" and potential divorce.

Verse 16 says that because of Eve's disobedience to God and her disrespect of her husband, the curse would now make her want to control him. Before the curse she had a desire to surrender, respect, and support Adam. After, her drive, default, and internal bent would now be to take charge, resist, and disrespect him.

Verse 16 also says that because Adam gave away His God-given leadership role when he listened to her instead of obeying Him (v. 17), he would now, instead of being loving, kind, and gentle towards Eve, have a drive, a default, and an internal bent to be harsh, cruel, and self-centered in his role as head (v. 16b).

Genesis 3 was a game changer for us. Seeing what took place back there and the marital messes it created helped Laurie and I make sense of what we had been struggling through for so many years. As we started to use Gen 3 as the starting point for explaining the problems we were having, it made it easier to understand where they were coming from and why they were happening. It also made it easier to forgive each other and to talk through why we kept doing what we kept doing. Because Laurie and I now had a concrete, biblical answer for where and why we continued to struggle, it gave us the ability to be more patient and forgiving with each other. It was no longer about our past, personality differences, or parents, but about what God said would happen in our marriage because of what He pronounced on Adam and Eve.

Now that we understood where our problems were coming from, we needed some guidance to help us biblically work through the marital repercussions from the curse. The answers we were looking for were found in Eph 5.

Ephesians 5:21–33

As I said earlier, I had for years (even after remarriage) continued to be rude, harsh, controlling, and angry towards Laurie. It wasn't until about five years ago as I was reading the Bible with Sammy that I came across Eph 5. Something (I believe it was God) seemed to be saying that I needed to spend more time in this chapter. I didn't get anything from it at first. But as I kept reading and questioning, it seemed like God was telling me through Paul that Eph 5 had the answers to the questions Laurie and I had of how to biblically work through the problems passed on to us by the curse.

The first helpful insight came from verse 21 when it said, "And further, submit to one another out of reverence for Christ." This verse explained to us that our being able to work through our marital problems would first be about our relationship and respect for Jesus, not the love and respect we did or didn't have for each other. Even if we didn't want to change for each other, we could use Jesus' love for us and our respect for Him as motivation to "be courteously reverent to one another" (v. 21 MSG).

Next (and I'm only looking at Laurie's curse issues first because that's how it's arranged in the chapter), verses 22 and 24 say, "For wives, this means submit to your husbands as to the Lord," and "Wives should submit to your husbands in everything." There it was. God's answer for Laurie's challenges of being controlling and disrespectful (because of the curse) was for her to respect me just like she respects Jesus. It was a spiritual trade-off: instead of showing sinful control and disrespect, out of love and respect for

Jesus, she could now (in His power) show respect and submit to me.

Next, verses 25 and 28 say, "For husbands, this means love your wives, just as Christ loved the church. He gave up his life for her," and "In the same way, husbands ought to love their wives as they love their own bodies." Finally! God's answer for my sins of being angry, harsh, and controlling was for me to love her just like Jesus loved the church. This was my spiritual trade-off: instead of showing sinful anger and harshness, out of love and respect for Jesus, I could (in His power) now show love and kindness by giving my life for her.

Lastly, God's answer for both of us, for overcoming the two main negative marital effects from the curse, in a nutshell was, "So again I say, each man must love his wife as he loves himself, and the wife must respect her husband" (v. 33).

This all seems so clear now. But back then, when we were trying so many superficial techniques and practices (that never addressed our core problems brought on by the curse), we got confused, frustrated, and were losing hope. Ephesians 5 brought clarity, direction, energy, and renewed hope for us and our marriage.

This new information created another problem. As I was attempting to put Eph 5 into practice, I couldn't figure out how I was supposed to give my life for Laurie in the same way Jesus gave His for the church. This is what we're going to look at in the next section.

Giving Our Lives for Our Wives

"FOR HUSBANDS, THIS MEANS love your wives, just as Christ loved the church. He gave up his life for her" (Eph 5:25). I believe God gave me the insight that Eph 5 was the answer to the two main problems Laurie and I had been working through. What it didn't do was give me the specifics of how to do it. The more time I spent reading chapter 5 and thinking through it, the more vague the passage became.

I understood that I was supposed to love Laurie the way Jesus loved His church. But how? Where were the details, the how-tos of actually doing it? Each time I read, "He gave up his life for her," the "gave" kept bothering me. I didn't know how to do it.

The first part of the answer seemed to be found in verses 1 and 2 of Eph 5. "Watch what God does, and then you do it, like children who learn proper behavior from their parents. Mostly what God does is love you. Keep company with him and learn a life of love. Observe how Christ loved us. His love was not cautious but extravagant. He didn't love in order to get something from us but to give everything of himself to us. Love like that" (MSG).

These verses were helpful in pointing me in the right direction. But now I needed to find a place in the Bible that would give me the ability to "watch" what Jesus did, and "observe" how Jesus "gave." I needed a biblical movie or documentary that detailed specifically, what, and why Jesus did what He did for His church.

The second (and main) part of the answer to my question was provided by Isa 53.

Nothing New

BEFORE WE LOOK AT Isa 53, I want to try and get across one more time how really hard and painful this is going to be. I'm even now going to ask God to give you the ability, courage, and passion to follow through with being crushed and grieved if that is His good plan for you. What you're about to hear is not going to be easy to hear.

The subtitle of this book suggests that there's an "old" and "new" facet to this method of marriage restoration. The "old" refers to God crushing and grieving Jesus in order to restore His marriage to His bride, the church. The "new," refers to what God through Paul is telling us to do: give our lives for our wives, in the same way Jesus did. So, in a sense, this isn't new either. God's method of marriage restoration has been around for over two thousand years.

It was God's good plan to crush and grieve Joseph in an Egyptian jail in order "to save His people from starvation" (Ps 105:17 TLB); it was God's good plan to crush and grieve Jesus on a Roman cross in order to save His people from their sin (Matt 1:21); and it may be God's good plan to crush and grieve you on the altar of your marriage (Rom 12:1; Eph 5:25–27) in order to save it.

What's coming up next is not new. It's unwanted, unasked for, scary, and impossible (on our own). But it's not new. This has been God's will for many Christian husbands for a very long time. The question is, has God got us in a place where He can use Jesus' sufferings for us, as an example and motivation, along with His empowering, to give us the ability to give to our wives in the same way He gave to us and His church outlined in Isaiah 53?

Isaiah 53

Isaiah 53 was the biblically historic documentary I was looking for. There are many general examples of how Jesus loved in the New Testament and many general directives throughout the Bible of how Christians are supposed to love. But Isa 53 fills in the specific pieces that were missing from Eph 5, showing us how to give as Jesus "gave."

It reads,

> Who believes what we've heard and seen? Who would have thought God's saving power would look like this?
>
> The servant grew up before God—a scrawny seedling, a scrubby plant in a parched field. There was nothing attractive about him, nothing to cause us to take a second look. He was looked down on and passed over, a man who suffered, who knew pain firsthand. One look at him and people turned away. We looked down on him, thought he was scum. But the fact is, it was our pains he carried—our disfigurements, all the things wrong with us. We thought he brought it on himself, that God was punishing him for his own failures. But it was our sins that did that to him, that ripped and tore and crushed him—our sins! He took the punishment, and that made us whole. Through his bruises we get healed. We're all like sheep who've wandered off and gotten lost. We've all done our own thing, gone our own way. And God has piled all our sins, everything we've done wrong, on him, on him.
>
> He was beaten, he was tortured, but he didn't say a word. Like a lamb taken to be slaughtered and like a sheep

being sheared, he took it all in silence. Justice miscarried, and he was led off— and did anyone really know what was happening? He died without a thought for his own welfare, beaten bloody for the sins of my people. They buried him with the wicked, threw him in a grave with a rich man, Even though he'd never hurt a soul or said one word that wasn't true.

Still, it's what God had in mind all along, to crush him with pain. The plan was that he give himself as an offering for sin so that he'd see life come from it—life, life, and more life. And God's plan will deeply prosper through him.

Out of that terrible travail of soul, he'll see that it's worth it and be glad he did it. Through what he experienced, my righteous one, my servant, will make many "righteous ones," as he himself carries the burden of their sins. Therefore I'll reward him extravagantly—the best of everything, the highest honors—Because he looked death in the face and didn't flinch, because he embraced the company of the lowest. He took on his own shoulders the sin of the many, he took up the cause of all the black sheep. (Isa 54:1–12 MSG).

If we were reading this and only read the first nine and a half verses, it would be reasonable to think that Jesus didn't seem to accomplish anything other than get ignored, disrespected, beat up, bloodied, and killed. Whatever He was trying to do, these verses seem to say that He failed.

But the next two and a half verses tell a much different story. God gives us His surprise ending and proclaims Jesus the overwhelming Victor. Not a loser He distanced Himself from, but a proud Father Who called Him "Mine,"[1] three times in less than two verses. Jesus accomplished everything God's "good plan" for Him was designed to accomplish. And to such a degree that God showered Jesus with extravagant rewards, "Because He looked death in the face and didn't flinch" (v. 10–12 MSG).

So much of the time God's ways don't match with ours (Isa 55:8–9), and most of the time don't look anything like the plans,

---

1. "My" in the MSG translation.

hopes, and dreams we may have had (including the ones we may have had for our marriage). But His plans and methods are always better than ours, no matter how bizarre, scary, or impossible they look. "Who *would've believed* what we've heard and seen *here?* Who would have thought God's [*marriage*] saving power would look like this?"[2] But it does look like this. It looked like this for Jesus and there's a high likelihood it could for you as well.

It's so common (I hope) for us to be grateful that Jesus went through all this when He suffered and died on the cross for us. It's a whole lot harder to believe He could be calling us to do the same thing. But this passage combined with Eph 5 are telling us to do just that: give our lives for our wives in the same way Jesus gave His for His bride, the church.

2. Author's paraphrase of verse 1.

A Helpful Way to Look at Isaiah 53

THERE'S A LOT GOING on in Isa 53. If we try to directly apply the sufferings Jesus endured for us and His church, there's a good chance we'll get confused, scared, and possibly give up. The worst of Jesus' suffering was not the physical torture and His eventual death by crucifixion but having all the world's sin placed on Him and being abandoned and forsaken by God (for a time) because of our sin (Ps 22; Matt 27:47; 1 John 2:1–2).

There's no way we could endure or do exactly what Jesus did (Heb 2:14–15). But He can and will do Isa 53 through us. The reason we know this is because He directed us to do it. As we talked about earlier, God never tells us to do anything that He isn't prepared to do in, through, and for us (John 15:4–8).

Initially it was challenging and somewhat confusing to look at what Jesus did here and translate that into my marriage. It came together for me, while reading and thinking through the passage to look at individual phrases and ask the Holy Spirit (John 16:12–13) to point out how I could apply Isa 53 to what was going on in Laurie's and my marriage. God, Jesus, and the Holy Spirit are All so loving and kind. They're All in this with us. We're not alone. They're here to not just point out where we need help, but to give it as well.

The phrases I believe God made important to me may not be the same ones the Holy Spirit points out to you. It might also be helpful as you're doing this exercise to ask God to give you the ability to be compassionate and kind to your wife as you're attempting to put it into practice (Eph 4:31–32). Jesus is always kind to us in our weakness and inabilities. We'll want to ask Him to give us His heart in order to behave like Him towards our wives as we're attempting to put Isa 53 into practice (Matt 12:20a).

Here's an example of some of the phrases that stuck out for me:

1. *Who would have thought God's saving power would look like this?* We've already touched on this a bit. But this thought from Isaiah can be helpful in getting us past the initial fear of what we're most likely going to go through. Reminding ourselves that even though we may be feeling overwhelmed, confused, weak, and relationally beat up, what we're going through is exactly what it should look like. It is God's good plan and His saving power that will be on display, even if it doesn't look or feel like we expected.

   As we looked at earlier; this method is not what most of us signed up for. Not many of us would have come up with this method on our own. Which one of us would have chosen suffering, service, and self-sacrifice as a means of restoring our marriage? But the biblical truth is, God's saving power for the world, His church, and for many of our marriages looks just like this.

2. *He was looked down on and passed over.* We have a tendency (I know I do) to take for granted, pass over, and even get comfortable with what Jesus went through in order to rescue us. It's much more difficult to accept that it may be God's "good plan" and method for us to go through similar difficulties, in order to rescue our marriages.

3. *A man who suffered, who knew pain firsthand.* It's likely, because you're reading this, that you are experiencing suffering and pain. It's horrible when we're in the middle of it. But, it's far worse when we don't understand why; think we're the only one whose ever had to go through it; and get stuck in the lie, believing that we're going through it alone and on our own. Jesus went through far worse ahead of us and will be with us as we follow His example (Is 43:1–2). Nahum 1:7 says, "The

LORD is good, a strong refuge when trouble comes. He is close to those who trust in him."

4. *We looked down on him, thought he was scum.* I remember walking into places that (before my divorce) showed respect, listened to my ideas, and even asked me to speak and preach. After, I remember a common theme when I walked into those same places: people would either whisper, laugh, or walk away. It was very discouraging and humbling. There was a time when it seemed and felt like I was a very second-class citizen. This not only applied to various ministries, but to family and friends as well. What I went through is nothing compared to what Jesus experienced. It can be helpful to remember that as we're possibly being looked down on and disrespected, Jesus went through the same thing before and for us.

5. *It was our pains he carried . . . and that made us whole.* This phrase helped me see a bit more clearly what it meant for me to give in the same way Jesus "gave" in verses 25–27 of Eph 5. Jesus carried my pains (including the pain of my sin, character flaws, family upbringing, and years of poor choices) and is now telling me to do the same thing for Laurie with the hope and goal of making her more spiritually whole and healthy.

    Just a thought: I wonder if it might make our giving to our wives easier if we could look at the "spots," "blemishes," and spiritual "wrinkles" of our wives (Eph 5:27) as pains she has been carrying? What if we like Jesus could lighten her load by forgiving, loving, and accepting her in the middle of our experiencing these spiritual blemishes? Jesus made us "whole" and "healed" when He did this for us. It can be a real encouragement to remember this, and ask Him to (even in the slightest way) use us to do the same for our wives.

6. *We're all like sheep who've wandered off and gotten lost.* This is true of us as well as our wives. We're all like sheep. Jesus says of Himself that one of the characteristics of being the Good Shepherd is His willingness to give His life for His sheep. "I am the good shepherd. The good shepherd gives His life for

the sheep" (John 10:11). Jesus can give us the ability and the heart of a kind shepherd just like Him. The key here might be to ask God to give us the ability to treat her as a wayward sheep, not a defiant enemy.

7. *We've all done our own thing, gone our own way.* Independence, lack of respect and various forms of defiance can be common (but many times unidentified) repercussions of the curse for our wives. Knowing this can make it easier to understand, forgive, and work through these potential difficulties. The pain and possible insecurities on our part will still have to be worked through. But remembering that she's not the only one who wandered off, that you and I have done it as well, might make it easier to be merciful and kind as we work through this exercise.

8. *And God has piled all our sins, everything we've done wrong, on him.* When someone does something wrong, someone has to pay for it. Thank God, Jesus not only paid for our sins and wrongs, but our wives' as well (Rom 6:23).

9. *He was beaten, he was tortured.* Realistically this is not going to happen to us. But there will be many times when it will feel like it. As we're going to see, what God has called us to do for our wives (possibly while in the middle of conflict, confusion, distance, and even divorce) is to endure various forms of marital suffering. But again, we're not trailblazers and certainly not alone.

10. *But he didn't say a word.* This will not be the same as the MNTR. There will be times when remaining silent will be an act of love. It will be painful, but a demonstration of God's love, nonetheless. Proverbs 17:9 says, "Love forgets mistakes; nagging about them parts the best of friends" (TLB).

I can see how this could come across as confusing; so let me share with you what I believe God has shown me. It's important when working through the MNTR not to remain silent when something needs to be said. At the same time, to keep harping on a sin, character flaw, or struggle is only going to discourage her and most likely create relational and possibly marital distance. Once we've addressed whatever the issue is, it's far better to pray (in private) and encourage her by telling her (at a different time) that you see her (as we looked at earlier) as being incredibly loved by Jesus and completely forgiven (Luke 7:47–48). But, based on this phrase, there will be times that the most loving and sacrificial thing we can do is remain silent.

11. *Justice miscarried.* It's going to feel as if so much of what we're experiencing is unfair. And many times, it will be. But we have Jesus' example to follow. Every time we continue to love and serve in the middle of being treated unfairly, God is pleased with us. First Peter 2:19–20 says, "A man does something valuable when he endures pain, as in the sight of God, though he knows he is suffering unjustly. After all, it is no credit to you if you are patient in bearing a punishment which you have richly deserved! But if you do your duty and are punished for it and can still accept it patiently, you are doing something worthwhile in God's sight" (Phillips).

God being pleased with us will mean so much more when it is His approval, His applause, His "at-a-boy" that motivates and energizes us, instead of the idolatrous need we may have to be appreciated or respected by our wives (John 5:41–44). The reason this is so necessary is that there will be many times (depending on how distanced we are from our wives) that we will not be receiving any encouragement or approval from her. And that'll have to be okay. We need His slap on the back, not hers during these difficult times.

One of the worst mindsets we can allow ourselves to get stuck in is self-pity. Feeling sorry for ourselves sucks God's energy and His joy out of us. As we remember that Jesus wasn't treated fairly as He was getting crushed and grieved, it'll make it easier to stay away from this negative self-talk and keep moving forward in faithfulness and obedience.

12. *Did anyone really know what was happening?* There will be many days when we'll feel like we're losing our minds. The pain will be so intense and may have been going on for so long, that we will be beside ourselves and possibly overwhelmed with confusion. God and Jesus know exactly what we're going through and why. We'll want to ask Them for the ability to keep our eyes of faith on Them, not our mixed-up emotions or negative marital circumstances. One of the phrases I think God gave me that has been a real calming agent for me is "he's in the back of the boat" (paraphrase of Mark 4:35–41). It's so easy to get overwhelmed and confused when we fixate on the fear-filled marital wind and waves. We can gain a lot of courage and persistence from remembering that even if we don't know what's happening, He does—and He's right there with us, right in the back of the boat.

13. *He died without a thought for his own welfare.* This goes back to our getting stuck in self-pity or unhealthy introspection. If we get stuck focusing on only what we can see (apart from God's perspective and plan) and the pain we're experiencing, it'll make what we're going through far worse. It can go a long way, in keeping us from getting stuck in self-pity, if we ask God to give us the ability to remember that we're doing what He wants, that this is His plan, and that He (even if she may not be) is pleased with us.

It will be nearly impossible for us to go through God's crushing and grieving and not have thoughts for our own welfare, unless its foundation is built on the truth that God loves us, is far wiser than us, and is totally in control of all our circumstances (Rom 8:31–39; 1 Cor 3:19; Ps 115:3).

If we're fixated on how our wives are treating us and that we need to win, and might somehow lose (no one ever wins in divorce), we won't be able to stop thinking about our welfare. If we're stuck in worry and fear about what a divorce might cost, we'll be overwhelmed with thoughts of our own welfare. If we allow ourselves to be more concerned about our welfare instead of God getting glorified, we won't be able to follow Jesus' example in this area of Isa 53.

Side note: glorifying God is kind of a big church word that basically means that God gets seen as good and amazing as He really is. One way that He gets glorified is when we obey Him. He gets seen even more clearly (glorified) when we obey Him in those areas that are too big for us and the world recognizes there was no way that we could have done what we did unless God, Jesus, and the Holy Spirit were the Ones who did it through us (Acts 4:8–13).

It's natural to have a drive for social, financial, and relational self-preservation. But God and Jesus are not directing us to do what comes natural with their directives in Eph 5 and Isa 53. God will be glorified, and we'll have a much better shot at getting our marriages back as we (in God's power), allow Him to give us the ability to let go of what comes naturally and trust in what comes natural to Him, miraculous interventions.

Side note: there was a day, during my divorce, that I was overwhelmed and came very close to taking my own life. I had to call my long-time discipler and best friend, Steve, and tell him about my mental and emotional condition. If you have lost hope and the ability to think of your own physical well-being, please don't hesitate; dial 911 if necessary and get the help you need.

God isn't asking us to lose our physical lives over our marital struggles. But here, He's giving us an example of thinking of others (in this case our wives and marriages), as more important than what we could gain or might lose because of the difficulties our marriages might be costing us (Phil 2:3).

In the middle of those times that seem to be so against us and aren't at all what we had hoped for our marriage, God has promised us that His joy can and will be what gets us through. His joy in these times really is our strength (Neh 8:10).

14. *For the sins of my people.* Jesus got crushed and grieved for our sins. We and our wives are whole, pure, and holy because

of Him (Col 1:22). As we keep in mind what His sacrifice accomplished for us, there's a far better chance we'll (in His power) be able to keep suffering, serving, and sacrificing for the misbehaviors and sins of our wives.

15. *Still, it's what God had in mind all along.* This is so important to remember as we're going through the pain. Pain without a reason or destination is unbearable. But, if we ask God to help us remember and accept that being crushed and grieved was His "good plan" for Jesus, it'll go a long way in keeping us from allowing unhelpful self-talk that's telling us what we're going through "isn't fair," that "this all must be a mistake or our unlucky misfortune," but what God had planned all along. Hebrews 12:2 says, "We do this by keeping our eyes on Jesus, the champion who initiates and perfects our faith. Because of the joy awaiting him, he endured the cross, disregarding its shame. Now he is seated in the place of honor beside God's throne." We'll want to keep our eyes on Jesus, Who, no matter how our marriage restoration efforts turn out, is perfecting us as we (in His power) continue to carry (as we're going to see later) the marital crosses He has designed for us carry.

16. *To crush him with pain.* It will be hard at times to surrender to the reality that our loving God's method for restoring our marriages is to crush us with pain. But Isa 53 gives us biblical evidence that God lovingly did this to His Son, and for many of us will lovingly and compassionately do this to and for us, for the sake of our marriages.

17. *So that he'd see life come from it—life, life, and more life.* What comes to mind here is John 10:10: "I came so they can have real and eternal life, more and better life than they ever dreamed of" (MSG). It seems God has a principle; whenever He takes something away or puts us through something difficult, He always gives us something better to replace what we've lost or matures us because of what we went through. Acts 3:19–20 says, "Now repent of your sins and turn to God, so that your sins may be wiped away. Then times of refreshment will come

from the presence of the Lord, and he will again send you Jesus, your appointed Messiah."

Another couple of verses that God gave me in advance of Laurie and I getting remarried was Joel 2:25–26. "I will give you back what you lost . . . and you will praise the Lord your God who *did this miracle* for you."[1]

As we give up our dreams (and possibly sinful demands) of an easy and comfortable marriage, God will give us times of refreshing that will consist of His promised "life in all its fullness" (John 10:10 TLB), whether He restores our marriages or not.

18. *And God's plan will deeply prosper through him.* This phrase gives us biblical reason to hope. We'll want to keep asking, seeking, and knocking for God to restore our marriages (Matt 7:7–8). But a really encouraging truth that is on our side is that God wants marriages to stay intact (Matt 19:6). There's something very encouraging and empowering, when we know that we are praying God's will into our life and marriage. First John 5:13–15 says, "And we are confident that he hears us whenever we ask for anything that pleases him. And since we know he hears us when we make our requests, we also know that he will give us what we ask for."

God's good plan prospered for Jesus in His efforts to restore His broken relationship with His bride, the church. Because of this, there's reason for hope that it can and will work for you as well. Whether it works or not, there's a whole lot more joy and energy that comes from following God's plan than being like wayward, independent sheep, following our own path (Isa 53:6).

19. *Out of that terrible travail of soul, he'll see that it's worth it and be glad he did it.* Terrible travail of soul sounds like something most of us would want to stay away from. But Paul, like Jesus, saw value in suffering and actually asked to have it be a part of his life and relationship with Jesus (Phil 3:9–10). Paul

1. Author's paraphrase.

earlier in Phil 1:29 said, "There's far more to this life than trusting in Christ. There's also suffering for him. And the suffering is as much a gift as the trusting" (MSG).

I know this is hard to talk about, but as we saw earlier, suffering, sacrifice, and here, travail of the soul, are all common experiences in the Christian life; and based on Eph 5, marriage as well. God will, and I hope already has, placed in us a desire to be like Him, be close to Him, and follow His example even if it means extreme suffering. Jesus said, "If anyone serves Me, he must [continue to faithfully] follow Me [without hesitation, holding steadfastly to Me, conforming to My example in living and, if need be, suffering or perhaps dying because of faith in Me]; and wherever I am [in heaven's glory], there will My servant be also. If anyone serves Me, the Father will honor him" (John 12:26 AMPC; brackets in the original).

As Jesus' disciples, He can give us the desire to follow the example He gave in Eph 5 and here in Isa 53 and recognize that the terrible sufferings we may go through for our marriages will be worth it and we'll be glad we did it.

20. *Through what he experienced, my righteous one, my servant will make many "righteous ones."* This phrase tells us why Jesus experienced "what He experienced"; to "make many righteous ones." Or for our purposes, "to make her holy and clean" (Eph 5:26). This is also why we'll want to ask God to give us the ability and supernatural desire to go through similar experiences for our wives and marriages.

Well, there's an example of what we can do to think through the phrases from Isa 53. This is not an easy exercise, and even harder when we actually put what's in our head or what we placed on paper into our struggling marriages. But again, God knew this would work for Jesus, and in the words from Lam 3:21, we'll have a good reason to "dare to hope" that He'll do the same for us.

Completely Doable

YOU MAY BE SAYING to yourself that, "God, Jesus, and Paul are asking too much! Isaiah 53 is impossible; there's no way." I understand. I completely agree with you. You and I can't do it. None of us can. But the good news is, He can and will.

The fear and anxiety you may be experiencing could be an indicator that you're trusting in yourself instead of God to do this through you. God may be using the memory of the times in the past that you attempted (on your own) to love when you felt unloved, to forgive when you felt judged, and to let go of resentments when you felt they were justified. All these (and others) could be God's gracious gift to us, to get us to stop looking to ourselves and look to Him instead.

Looking to ourselves is an instant recipe for failure. If we are the only ones in the equation, we're going to fail. But, when Jesus is added, nothing is impossible (Luke 1:37; Phil 4:13). But again, the wonderful truth is that God never asks or tells us to do anything that He hasn't already done (in one form or another) and isn't going to do in, through and for us (Mark 11:23; Gal 2:20; Col 1:29; Zech 4:6). Deuteronomy 31:8 says, "Do not be afraid or discouraged, for the Lord will personally go ahead of you. He will be with you; he will neither fail you nor abandon you."

Jesus is talking about His impending death, burial, and resurrection in John 12:23–26. Verse 24 can be helpful in attempting to understand what it's going to take to get us out of the "me" equation and get Him in. It reads, "I tell you the truth, unless a kernel of wheat is planted in the soil and dies, it remains alone. But its death will produce many new kernels—a plentiful harvest of new lives." Our egos, and our "I just have to believe in myself" mindset have to be planted in the ground and allowed to die. When God makes this possible (which will most likely take place as God exposes our continued failures), His new, Gal 2:20 life sprouts up. We're now out of the way and He's now engaged. This spiritual process of our being planted in difficult situations (such as our struggling marriage), in order to get us to die to our self-reliance, makes the doing of Eph 5 and Isa 53 completely doable when He is the One that is raised to new life in us.

Here's one last example that might help with our fears of living out Isa 53 and Eph 5. It is found in Matt 11:28–30. "Then Jesus said, 'Come to me, all of you who are weary and carry heavy burdens, and I will give you rest. Take my yoke upon you. Let me teach you, because I am humble and gentle at heart, and you will find rest for your souls. For my yoke is easy to bear, and the burden I give you is light.'"

Thinking about my need to give my life for my wife in the same way Jesus gave His for us is a heavy and impossible burden to carry. But here Jesus is telling us that He will give us rest from our burdens. One of the reasons His yoke is easy and the burdens He gives us are light is because He's the One doing all the pulling. He does the work. It's not inactivity on our part, but supernatural activity on His.

This for most of us is completely foreign to how we've been taught and how we've lived our lives. We're not comfortable with handouts; we've learned and have become very comfortable with pulling our own weight. The problem with this is it doesn't work. God isn't seen as good and powerful as He is (glorified) if He were to assign us tasks that we can do without Him. This is why Paul could say of his weakness, "So now I am glad to boast about my weaknesses, so that the power of Christ can work through me. That's why I take pleasure in my weaknesses, and in the insults, hardships, persecutions, and troubles that I suffer for Christ. For when I am weak, then I am strong" (2 Cor 12:9b–10).

What's being asked of us in Eph 5 and Isa 53 is completely impossible—on our own. But completely doable as He teaches us to let go of our anemic self-reliance and let Him do it through us.

A Helpful Marital Exercise

ANOTHER WAY TO APPLY what Jesus suffered in Isa 53 is by using this simple exercise. Because it would be difficult for me to connect with each and every personal situation or difficulty you're experiencing, it's my hope that this exercise will give you the ability to do the connecting yourself.

The exercise works like this: as you read the chapter, place yourself into whatever Jesus was doing, thinking, or feeling while being crushed and grieved. Think through the problems you and your wife are having and ask the Holy Spirit to give you ideas of how you can place Jesus' acts of suffering, service, and self-sacrifice into your marriage.

Next, as you are reading, whenever you see "we," "us," "our," "us all," "no one," "many," or "many descendants" (NLT), imagine the person being described as your wife. For example, mentally picture her doing what was done ("All of us like sheep have strayed away," v. 6) or how she may have responded ("We turned our backs on him and looked the other way. He was despised, and we did not care," v. 3b), or how your being crushed and grieved benefited her ("For many to be counted righteous, for he will bear all their sins," v. 11b).

And finally, imagine yourself reacting to your wife's growth and positive change in the same way Jesus responded, with gladness and a sense of worthwhile accomplishment (v. 11).

None of us (apart from God's grace) want to be crushed and grieved. But as we gain new insights of how to specifically give our lives for our wives after using this exercise, and see God making supernatural changes in her, we will, like Jesus, be grateful and "satisfied" with what He has "accomplished" in our marriages.

Suffering, Self-Sacrifice, and Service

Dr. Josef Tson was one of the first guest chapel speakers I remember during my first year at Bible college. His stories of being captured, imprisoned, and tortured by Communists in Romania were unforgettable.

In his book, *Suffering, Martyrdom and Rewards in Heaven*, Dr. Tson presents a biblical case for the importance of incorporating suffering (and possibly martyrdom) into the relationships and ministries God has given us. His thoughts in this area can be applied to marriage. Dr. Tson writes, "The first duty of the disciple is, therefore, to discover the will of his Master and to do it with joy and passion."[1]

God's will for us is to give our lives for our wives. A practical way to accomplish this is through suffering, service, and self-sacrifice. This goes along with what we saw in Isa 53.

For most of us, God hasn't designed that we sacrifice our physical life for our wives. Our sufferings will take the form of daily surrenderings, humblings, or sacrifices that might take the form of praying for—instead of pointing out problems, or simply showing acts of love when we're feeling unloved or disrespected.

There have been times while reading the Bible that what I'm reading seems to be "the will of my Master" for my marriage, but either seems too difficult to do, or I'm not exactly sure what He's wanting to say. I've found that if I ask God to make me faithful, to not give up or let go of the tension, He many times shows me something new and gives me the desire to put it into practice with

1. Tson, *Suffering, Martyrdom*, 424.

51

Laurie. It's then (many times) that He gives me the "joy and enthusiasm" that Dr. Tson is talking about.

I didn't create these positive emotions, God did. This also goes along with the faithfulness that He provided. All this goes back to our understanding that we don't have what it takes, but He does, and He's willing to share. Matthew 5:3 says, "God blesses those who . . . realize their need for him."

Here are just a few passages that God used to help me "discover the will of *my* Master" in the context of my marriage and relating to Laurie. I won't be giving any major explanations for the verses, but instead just a short snippet of what seemed like God was trying to get me to notice:

1. For the most part I hope you and your wife never turn into actual enemies. But there will most likely be those times when neither of you feels like loving the other. Luke 6:27–36 clearly shows us our Master's will.

    > But to you who are willing to listen, I say, love your enemies! Do good to those who hate you. Bless those who curse you. Pray for those who hurt you. If someone slaps you on one cheek, offer the other cheek also. If someone demands your coat, offer your shirt also. Give to anyone who asks; and when things are taken away from you, don't try to get them back. Do to others as you would like them to do to you. If you love only those who love you, why should you get credit for that? Even sinners love those who love them! And if you do good only to those who do good to you, why should you get credit? Even sinners do that much! And if you lend money only to those who can repay you, why should you get credit? Even sinners will lend to other sinners for a full return. Love your enemies! Do good to them. Lend to them without expecting to be repaid. Then your reward from heaven will be very great, and you will truly be acting as children of the Most High, for he is kind to those who are unthankful and wicked. You must be compassionate, just as your Father is compassionate.

There's a lot going on here that is impossible for me to do unless Jesus is the One doing it through me. But, if He's told us to do it, then He will do it through us. First Thessalonians 5:24 says, "He who calls you is faithful, who also will do it" (NKJV).

Just a sidenote: the word "compassionate" is also translated "kind" in some translations. For some reason being kind to Laurie was easier for me than being compassionate.

2. God used John 13:1–5 in a really important way in my life. After spending some time in this passage (this is the one where Jesus washes the disciple's feet), I believe He made it clear to me that one of the ways I could show love to Laurie and Sammy was to serve them. I now see that she and Sammy are my number one ministry. God gives me joy when I alter my schedule in order to try to make life a little easier for Laurie or fill in when she needs a break or a hand with something.

3. God has used 1 Cor 13:4–7 numerous times in my marriage when I was being a self-centered narcissist, or possibly wanted to stop serving in something involving Laurie or Sammy. It reads, "Love is patient and kind. Love is not jealous or boastful or proud or rude. It does not demand its own way. It is not irritable, and it keeps no record of being wronged. It does not rejoice about injustice but rejoices whenever the truth wins out. Love never gives up, never loses faith, is always hopeful, and endures through every circumstance." He reminded me that this was His will for me at the very moment I needed it, and many times gave the desire, joy, and energy to keep loving and serving.

4. Matthew 23:11 is probably a verse we're pretty familiar with. But there's a huge difference between just remembering it and putting it into practice, especially if we're in the middle of feeling unloved, unserved, disrespected, or are moving towards a divorce. It reads, "The more lowly your service to others, the greater you are. To be the greatest, be a servant."

5. If we're stuck in marital idolatry (this is where we are more concerned about pleasing our wives than God), there's a good

chance we're not going to do what's being asked of us in Eph 5. Paraphrasing John 12:43 to fit our exercise here might look something like this: "For they loved the praise of *their wife* more than the praise of God."[2] Surrendering to God's will and looking for God's applause and approval, instead of hers, will go a long way in helping us accomplish what we covered earlier regarding our headship responsibilities.

6. This next verse goes along with the point we just covered. We're going to look at this more fully in the next section, but I wanted to share verse 26 from Luke 14 in the context of doing what Dr. Tson said was our "first duty" as one Jesus' disciple. It says, "Anyone who wants to be my follower must love me far more than he does his own wife . . . otherwise he cannot be my disciple."[3] This verse, in the context of Dr. Tson's knowing and doing God's will with joy and enthusiasm has made a huge difference in how I look at my relationship with Jesus as his disciple and how to prioritize my marriage more biblically.

Dr. Tson goes on to say, "God entered history by sending His Incarnate Son as a suffering slave who would end His own earthly life enduring torture and martyrdom. In this event, God revealed to us that suffering and self-sacrifice are His specific methods for tackling the problems of rebellion, of evil, and of the sin of mankind. Self-sacrifice is the only method consistent with His own nature."[4]

This next statement is going to come across as hard and unloving, but the biblical reality is, the by-products of the curse on our wives and ourselves is full of sin. This sin is going to result in harshness and anger on our part and rebellion and disrespect on hers. Keeping this in mind, as we're attempting to apply what Dr. Tson is suggesting here, we'll want to ask God to give us the ability to tackle the problems of rebellion, of evil, and of the sin that is present in our wives (please refer back to Gen 3 and Eph 5:26–27).

2. Author's paraphrase from TLB.
3. Author's paraphrase from TLB.
4. Tson, *Suffering, Martyrdom*, 425.

Since this is "the only method consistent with His own nature," we'll want to ask God to give us the ability to follow Jesus' example and directive from Luke 14:26.

Ephesians 5, then, won't be about "wearing the pants in the family," or demanding respect from our wives. It will be more about imitating Jesus' example and give our life for our wives. The potential rebellions, manipulations, and disrespect (along with other spiritual blemishes) can all be addressed as we imitate Jesus by surrendering and humbly following through (in His power), with God's good plan to crush and grieve us as we suffer, serve, and sacrifice for our wives. We'll want to ask God to give us a heart that is more concerned about her growth than we are about what it is costing us.

Biblically Hating Our Wives

IN ORDER FOR US to be able to follow through with the sufferings, services, and self-sacrifices that are going to be required of us to accomplish our God-directed, Eph 5 headship and husband responsibilities, we're going to need to love Jesus more than our wives.

Jesus in Luke 14:25–35 is talking to a group of potential disciples. He tells them what would be required of them as one of His close followers. He begins by saying, "If you want to be my disciple, you must, by comparison, hate everyone else" (v. 26).

In other passages He tells us to love, respect, honor, serve, and view others as more important than ourselves. But here He's telling us we need to hate all the important people in our life, in comparison to our love for Him. Or more simply, "You must love Me more than these." This is the first and primary criteria of following Jesus. It was true of the crowd that day and it is true for us as well.

There are seven important loves Jesus said needed to be hated. Because of the emphasis of this book, we're only going to focus on two: our wives, and later, our lives.

When I first started to take seriously (about five years ago) that I needed to hate Laurie in comparison to my love for Jesus, I got confused, frustrated, and angry. I didn't know it then (I do now), as we talked about earlier, I had made an idol of Laurie. She had become my first love, and Jesus had taken a relational back seat (this is a common and many times unidentified problem in marriages). But in my current state (back then) I wasn't even close to meeting this requirement to be one of Jesus' close followers.

I didn't like that He was exposing my sin of marital idolatry. And liked even less His process of undoing it. He helped me see that Laurie wasn't supposed to meet my needs the way I had for years expected her to. He allowed me to experience loneliness, depression, despair, and even thoughts of not wanting to live in order to help me see that Laurie wasn't my first love or primary need-meeter. The process was painful, but in the end, freeing. What initially felt like God killing me, was actually Him making it possible for me to be more dependent on Him, and less on Laurie. To just love her, instead of worshiping and placing unrealistic (and unbiblical) demands on her to be what only God was supposed to be in my marriage.

It was during this process that God graciously returned my first love for Him (Rev 2:4). It was like I got born again, again. These last few years have been the best of my life and marriage. It took God putting Jesus back in His rightful, first-love spot to make this happen.

Here in Luke 14, Jesus is telling us, that if we've gotten offtrack and are making a higher priority of our love for our wives instead of Him (not biblically hating her), we're going to have to repent and ask for His help to kindly and graciously depose her. If we want to be His disciple and follow His example of giving our lives for our wives, we're going to have to first hate her in comparison to our love for Him.

The Yes Test

YOU MIGHT ASK, "How can I tell if I love Him more than her?" An easy way to see where we're at in our love priorities is what could be called the yes test. If I say "yes" to her when I should've said "no," there's a problem. If I say "no" to Him, and "yes" to her when it should have been the other way around, my love is offtrack and I'm not biblically hating her as Jesus directed.

Jesus said, "I have loved you even as the Father has loved me. Remain in my love. When you obey my commandments, you remain in my love, just as I obey my Father's commandments and remain in his love" (John 15:9–10). Paraphrasing these two verses to fit this test looks like this: "I have loved you even as the Father has loved me. Remain in my love. When you say 'yes' to Me, instead of her, you've made Me your First Love, just as I say 'yes' to my Father and have made Him My First Love." This is a simple and practical way for us to recognize whether or not we are biblically hating our wives.

Hating Our Own Lives

THIS IS THE SECOND relationship we're going to look at from Luke 14. At the end of verse 26, Jesus tells the crowd (and us) that we're supposed to biblically hate our own lives. This is wonderfully interesting. This word "life" in the Greek is the word *psuche*.[1]

Psuche-life represents the self-identified thoughts and beliefs I have mentally and emotionally adopted, of what I believe I need for me to be me. Psuche-life says, "I am me because [fill in the blank]." What Jesus is saying here is that I can't be His disciple unless I "hate" what I had previously chose to believe I needed to make me, me.

Jesus telling us we'll need to hate our life can be applied to our marriages. Many of the problems and frustrations we're experiencing may stem from the psuche-life images we adopted before we got married. God uses difficulties and disappointments in our marriages to get us to "hate" or let go of our previously adopted marital-psuche-life images. This includes the hopes, dreams, and fantasies of what we believed we needed in marriage to satisfy and fulfill us. What we chose to believe we needed to make us, us, will now need to be hated, or loved less than what Jesus says will make us, us in our marriage; Him (and His will for us in our marriage), not what she would or could do for us.

An example of this can be found in what we previously looked at in Eph 5:25–26. Our premarital-psuche-life images most likely didn't include our God-assigned position of being the head of our wives and all the marital challenges that go with it.

1. Swanson, *Dictionary of Biblical Languages*.

But this God-directed ministry will now need to be included in our marital-psuche-life images and desires. Following through with God's good plan to crush and grieve us for the sake of our wives' spiritual growth will be what most satisfies and fulfills us; what makes us, us.

As we obey Him, and humbly (in His power) let go of previously held, marital-psuche-life beliefs, we'll be applying Jesus' directive to hate our own life and continue to qualify as one of His disciples.

Shouldering Our Marital Crosses

Luke 14:27 says, "Anyone who won't shoulder his own cross and follow behind me can't be my disciple" (MSG). We all have crosses to carry. Since God is in charge of everything in the universe, including directing the thoughts of the king (see Prov 21:1) and the roll of dice (Prov 16:33), He's also in charge of the crosses He's designed for us to carry.

The context of verse 27 is speaking directly to our responsibilities as Jesus' disciples. But this isn't just restricted to what's normally considered ministry. It can also apply to the ministry God has given us of discipling our wives.

Undoing the marital curse and helping our wives work through her spiritual spots and blemishes is one of our most important ministries. And since Jesus told us, in Eph 5, that this is His will for us, it's now one of the requirements of our being His disciple and a cross we'll need to carry.

We most likely didn't think about crosses before we got married. But cross-carrying is nonetheless included as an essential part of our role as head and husbands; a responsibility we'll hopefully take on with joy and enthusiasm (especially as we see our wives becoming more like Jesus and hopefully liking us more).

Jesus repeats this directive in Luke 14:33. "Whoever does not carry his own cross [expressing a willingness to endure whatever may come] and follow after Me [believing in Me, conforming to My example in living and, if need be, suffering or perhaps dying because of faith in Me] cannot be My disciple" (AMPC; brackets in the original).

Jesus is telling us to have a willingness to carry whatever crosses He designs. This will need to include the cross of being crushed and grieved. The word "gave" in Eph 5:25, is a cross carrying directive. Since we want to be Jesus' disciples in our marriage, the cross of helping our wives become holy, clean, and washed is one we're going to want to ask God to give us the ability to carry, "until death do us part."

Functional Cross-Carrying

GOD TOLD HOSEA TO, "Go marry a prostitute." He then said, "So that some of her [Gomer's] children will be conceived in prostitution" (Hos 1:2). Unless we'd seen it with our own eyes, we would've said that this doesn't sound like something God would say. But God had a plan and purpose for Hosea's life that was greater and worth more than the pain he would experience from it.

God's purpose for Hosea was to show a nation how unfaithful it had been to Him. God's purposes for our carrying our marital crosses will many times look and feel just as inconceivable as what Hosea went through. To continue to love our wives in the middle of the pain, possible resentments, and confusion may seem (for a time) worse than being told to marry a woman we know in advance, will be unfaithful.

If we're struggling in our marriage, it's not a mistake. It's God-directed. It's part of God's good plan to crush and grieve us for the sake of restoring or improving our marriages. We're going to want to stay away from thoughts that suggest He wouldn't have done this, or that He made a mistake. Because we are His disciples, we're going to want to trust and believe that He personally handcrafted the perfect crosses we'd need to carry in order to help our wives become more like Him.

No matter how unreasonable it may seem, we're going to want to ask Him to give us the ability to trust and believe that like Hosea, the pain we're experiencing is serving a higher purpose and goes beyond just the crushing and grieving we're experiencing.

The Consequences of Not Carrying Our Marital Crosses

VERSUS 34–35 IN LUKE 14 cap off Jesus' instructions to His potential disciples. "Therefore, salt is good; but if even salt has become tasteless, with what will it be seasoned? It is useless either for the soil or the manure pile, so it is thrown out. The one who has ears to hear, let him hear."

Jesus is telling the crowd (and us) what it'll cost if we choose to love our loved ones (including our wives) more than Him; to hang onto our adopted, self-satisfying images of what we believe we needed in order for us to be us; or to choose to abandon the crosses (including our difficult marriages) that He has designed for us. The cost is saltlessness. It won't be our salvation, forgiveness, love, or acceptance. It will be the loss of our opportunity for intimacy and the satisfaction and fulfillment of being used by Him. Heaven isn't in jeopardy. But our sitting on the spiritual sidelines till then will be.

If we choose the easy route of not fulfilling our God-directed role of discipling our wives, or abdicate our role of headship, or choose to leave (in whatever form that might take), we'll lose our saltiness. If we choose comfort over crosses, our saltiness will be gone.

We're going to have to adopt the belief that it's always better to carry our crosses than to drop them and run. Regret stinks. It sucks the life out of life and our marriages. Paul said in Acts 20:24, "But my life is worth nothing to me unless I use it for finishing the work assigned me by the Lord." Our lives will seem worth-less unless we faithfully use them to pick up and carry the marital crosses He has designed for us. Even if we don't understand why God is telling us to do the things we don't want to do, and the pain we're experiencing feels like it's going to kill us, we're going to want to ask Him to give us the ability to continue to carry our marital crosses and keep our salt.

In the Middle of the Crushing and Grieving, Keep Asking

HELPING OUR WIVES REMOVE the spiritual spots and blemishes passed on to them from Gen 3 is humanly impossible. Wanting to not start or quit will be frequent temptations. On those days, we'll need to keep asking God for His help. "And so I tell you, keep on asking, and you will receive what you ask for. Keep on seeking, and you will find. Keep on knocking, and the door will be opened to you. For everyone who asks, receives. Everyone who seeks, finds. And to everyone who knocks, the door will be opened" (Luke 11:9–10).

There will be many days during God's "good plan" of crushing and grieving, that it will seem as if heaven is shut, God's ears are closed, and He's either not listening or doesn't care. This is never true (1 Pet 5:7). What He's telling us to do in the middle of our marital cross carrying is to keep asking.

Grace

I KNOW I'VE SAID this before, but again, I can't make any guarantees. I can only tell you how it happened for us. For years Laurie and I had been struggling in our marriage (we're still working through things). But something happened a number of years ago. God hooked us up with an amazing, grace-oriented online church. With Sammy's medical challenges and compromised immune system, it's nearly impossible to be around others and keep Sammy healthy. So, our online church is perfect for us.

Our pastor has a checkered past (just like the rest of us). He believes and rests in God's grace (what He has done for him), enough to take the risk of being real about who he is and what God has done and is doing in his life. It's energizing for us to hear our pastor confessing his sins to us and others (Jas 5:16). Laurie, Sammy, and I have received spiritual healing and growth because of our pastor's authentic vulnerability.

We have experienced freedom, growth, and renewed energy from getting to know God and Jesus from a grace perspective. Our church's message makes it okay for Laurie and me to be broken and messed up, and be able to admit our messed upnesses and sins to each other. God is making us not only okay with our brokenness, but also able to accept each other in the broken ways we try to work through it.

Both Laurie and I have seen growth in our lives since we started "attending." But I have seen the greatest growth in Laurie. The change has been amazing. I'm not the easiest guy to be married to (Laurie would have no problem admitting this with a smile on her face). But since we started understanding God's grace, that He loves and accepts us, for free, whether we do it right or not (things Laurie and I have both longed for our entire lives); we're able to more freely and more frequently give these same gifts we received from God, to each other.

The change was easy to see in Laurie. In the past when she and I would try to work through something, I would get angry and say something stupid, and she would cry and leave the room. Now, she sticks in there, listens, cares, and lets me know she wants to be a friend by listening, even when I don't say or do it right. This, for me, has been a marriage-changer.

Another change has been her energy and attitude. I don't know how she does it, but she stays up at night with Sammy (due to his chronic medical needs) and gets so little sleep. Yet every morning she wakes up with a smile on her face, a happy greeting for me, and just looks gorgeous.

Grace energizes, while unacceptance sucks the life out of our wives and marriage. Grace says, "I love you just the way you are, not the way you or anyone else says you should be." Having the knowledge that we are good enough for Him and each other is both freeing and energizing.

Another benefit we've seen from our new understanding of grace is receiving the power and desire to do God's will. This is Jesus' Gal 2:20 life we talked about earlier. "I have been crucified with Christ; and it is no longer I who live, but Christ lives in me; and the life which I now live in the flesh I live by faith in the Son of God, who loved me and gave Himself up for me" (NASB). It's where Jesus (through the Holy Spirit) lives His supernatural life through us. This is what God and Jesus have been doing in Laurie ever since she's been exposed to and marinating in grace.

She's now so capable. It's unbelievable to see all she does around the house. She's been caring for Sammy for over twenty-five years. She does it with such joy, patience, and kindness. What she does throughout the day in taking care of Sammy and me is not humanly possible. Grace and Jesus' 2:20 life has given her the power and desire to do His will for our family and marriage.

It reminds me of that passage in 1 Cor 7 where Paul says a husband can be won over by his wife's Christlike attitude and character. Laurie has been winning me over with her grace-filled, in-love-with-Jesus, energized life.

Real change in marriage first takes place as God produces real change in our relationship with Him. When He becomes a higher priority to us than the relationship we do or don't have with our wives, He's then freed up to do whatever changes He thinks needs to take place in us and our marriages.

The marital change we're hoping for is going to revolve around grace. Grace is that thing that provides the only atmosphere where true change is possible. That atmosphere is unconditional love and acceptance; first from Him, then by His grace, from us.

I'm Going to Show You How Much You Must Suffer

JESUS IN ACTS 9:16 says of Paul, "And now I'm about to show him what he's in for—the hard suffering that goes with this job" (MSG). This is also what many of us are in for, the hard suffering that goes along with the job God has given us of restoring our marriages.

God never wastes pain. He always does something good with it. It might be that He's using it to make us more like Him (Phil 1:6), to let us know we've gotten off course (Heb 12:5–9), to help us realize our dependence on Him (2 Cor 12:8–10), to help us better understand and experience His love (Rom 5:3–5), or to let us know we're not treating our wives as lovingly as He'd like (Mal 2:10–16; 1 Pet 3:7).

The point of this section is to help us see that difficulties and sufferings are both common tools God uses in the job He's given us of restoring our marriages. Our going through suffering doesn't mean we made a bad choice or are out of His will. We'll want to remember that Isa 53 illustrated for us that the suffering Jesus experienced was God's good plan for Him, and there's a really good chance it will be for many of us as well.

Having a Rich Relationship With God

IN THIS SECTION WE want to look at what Jesus said was needed in order to keep from getting distracted from our most treasured treasure; a rich relationship with God. We're going to look at Luke 12:13–34. The core, center, and hub of these verses is verse 21. It's also the core, center, and hub of the Christian life.

This passage shows how to keep from getting stuck in lust and greed, and how to stay away from trying to get our security needs met from acquiring possessions. And finally, how to keep from getting overwhelmed with anxiety, fear, and worry.

Here's an important thought to consider: if what I'm trusting in to meet my needs can be lost or taken away, it's not worthy of being my dearest treasure.

Verse 21 reads, "Yes, a person is a fool to store up earthly wealth but not have a rich relationship with God."

The Bible translators (at least in the NLT) inserted the word "wealth." It's not in the original manuscripts. The NASB says, "So is the man who stores up treasure for himself, and is not rich toward God." So "storing up" isn't just limited to wealth but can include anything we might want to store up or treasure.

A treasure is anything or anyone we choose to place our trust in, to make us feel the way we want to feel: secure, significant, comfortable, or in control. All these are fool's gold. They look treasurable, but are worthless in comparison to a rich relationship with God (Phil 3:7–8). The verse can more accurately read, "Yes a person is a fool to store up [fill in the blank], but not have a rich relationship with God."

Because of this more accurate reading, we can add marriage and our relationship with our wives as one of the things we might want to "store up" and treasure more than our rich relationship with God.

Looking at the big picture from this passage: the man in verses 13–14 treasured and wanted to get (store up) his inheritance, believing it would make him feel the way he wanted to feel: secure, full, and complete. The man in verses 15–20 treasured storing up grain (possessions), believing this would make him feel the way he wanted to feel: comfortable and secure. And finally, the folks in verses 22–34 treasured and wanted to acquire (store up) daily essentials like food and clothing, believing if they could get these on their own, they would feel the way they wanted to feel: capable, self-sufficient, and in control. They believed that if they had these things, they would no longer feel what they were feeling, "concerned" and "worried" (v. 29).

From these three examples Jesus gives at least three important insights:

1.   We need to have a rich relationship with God.

2.   If we don't have this relationship, we will treasure other smaller-than-God things (idols) to fill that void.

3.   If we do number 2, we're going to get offtrack and struggle in life with greed, lust, anxiety, fear, and worry.

I recently stained our fence and deck. I made the mistake of purchasing the wrong color. The label said "redwood," but after I applied it, looked more like orangish pumpkin instead of the rich, satisfying color I'd hoped for. Every time I saw it, it made me feel disappointed and sad. The color I ended up getting instead is rich. It is deep, full, and comforting. It makes me feel the way I'd hoped I would whenever I see it. This is what a rich relationship with God looks like. It fills us up, completes us, and makes us feel the way, deep down inside, we want to feel: full.

Psalms 16 describes what experiencing a rich relationship with God is like. "In Your presence is fullness of joy; In Your right hand there are pleasures forever" (v.11 NASB). Fullness of joy and pleasure feels good, wholesome, and fulfilling: just the way we long to feel on a daily basis.

If I choose to look to other things or other relationships to compensate for my not having a rich relationship with God, I'll end up feeling empty, anxious, and full of fear, just like the people in these examples.

Verse 34 says, "Wherever your treasure is, there the desires of your heart will also be." Anything or anyone we choose to treasure before, more, or instead of our rich relationship with God is an idol. Similarly to what we looked at earlier, idols are smaller-than-God replacements we choose to run to because we either failed to treasure Him to begin with or got distracted by someone or something else. Second Corinthians 11:3 says, "But I fear that somehow your pure and undivided devotion to Christ will be corrupted, just as Eve was deceived by the cunning ways of the serpent." This is what trusting in idols does: they distract us from our rich relationship with God and Jesus.

Idols work. They work until they don't. But eventually they always don't. And when they stop working is when the worry, anxiety, fear, and other negative, debilitating thoughts and emotions take over.

Verse 34 also talks about our heart. The idea of heart in the Bible is talking about something far more substantial than what we feel or experience. It includes our mind, will, and emotions. It's like the driver's seat or command post of who we are. It's where our passion for life resides.

Proverbs 4:23 says that we're going to want to keep an intense guard over our heart. "Guard your heart above all else, for it determines the course of your life." And what we're guarding against is anything (our marriages), or anyone (our wives), that might take the place of our rich relationship with God. If He is not our Number One Passion, we'll lose our drive to live. We'll get confused, lost, and scared. We're going to want to ask God to help us guard our hearts and protect our rich relationship with Him, so that He stays our most treasured treasure.

Luke 12:33 says, "And the purses of heaven never get old or develop holes. Your treasure will be safe; no thief can steal it and no moth can destroy it." Like we talked about earlier, if what I'm choosing as my highest treasure can be taken or lost, it's not worthy of my treasuring. I'll be disappointed and crushed when it fails to do what I was trusting it to.

Obviously our wives and marriages can be lost. Therefore, we're going to want to ask God to be our most treasured treasure instead of her. In order for us to keep going and not quit, especially when she's not loving us, or it seems we're losing our marriage, what we treasured most (our rich relationship with God) will still be intact. We'll (in His power) be able to continue to love, even when we may be losing her and our marriages. This is why having a rich relationship with God is so important in our efforts to restore our marriages.

Complete and Utter Pardon

FORGIVING LOVE IS GOD'S primary means of freeing people. Grace transforms the condemned, from crushed and broken to renewed and alive. Complete and utter pardon instead of casting stones dissolves the burden of guilt and restores a passion for Him.

There's a picture of this thought in John 8:1–11. A woman was caught red-handed in a sin she should have been killed for. Skipping all the details, Jesus showed her forgiving love. He gave her complete and utter pardon by dissolving her burden of guilt through grace.

This is important. It will be very difficult to go through God's "good plan" if we're hanging onto resentments from past sins and hurts instead of showing forgiveness and grace. The resentments and unforgiveness we might be hanging onto could easily be sins that keep us from accomplishing God's Eph 5 will for us. "Let us strip off every weight that slows us down, especially the sin that so easily trips us up. And let us run with endurance the race God has set before us" (Heb 12:1).

One of the ways we strip these sins is to recognize that God has forgiven us. Because we can only give what we've been given from God, we can now pass on this same forgiveness that will free her from being condemned, crushed, and broken to being renewed and alive. Our complete and utter pardon, instead of casting stones, will dissolve her burden of marital guilt and restore her passion for Him, and hopefully us, and our marriages.

Reading the Bible Together

"FOR HUSBANDS, THIS MEANS love your wives, just as Christ loved the church. He gave up his life for her to make her holy and clean, washed by the cleansing of God's word" (Eph 5:25–26).

There are many ways we can get the Bible into our marriages. The obvious and easiest is by reading it with our wives. Because God has given me the desire to take Eph 5 seriously, Laurie and I have started reading the Bible together. It's usually every night at around nine o'clock. It's something both of us look forward to (even though we're both really tired by then).

We set it up to be short so that it would be doable. We start the time off with a short and simple prayer, asking God to help us know Jesus better and have Him make His grace a bigger part of our life. We both believe that every time we open the Bible, God is going to do whatever life-changing thing He wants to do to and for us. Isaiah 55:11 says, "It is the same with my word. I send it out, and it always produces fruit. It will accomplish all I want it to, and it will prosper everywhere I send it."

We limited ourselves to reading for one minute and then discussing what we've read for three. It's amazing how much can be accomplished in this short amount of time. We usually go over the allotted time because we're both enjoying what we're getting. Recently, we're choosing books written by Paul, because of his simple and clear teachings on God's grace.

As we make a priority of loving and serving our wives, through spending time together reading the Bible, we will be fulfilling another portion of our Eph 5 responsibility of discipling our wives.

Conclusion

"After washing their feet, he put on his robe again and sat down and asked, 'Do you understand what I was doing? You call me "Teacher" and "Lord," and you are right, because that's what I am. And since I, your Lord and Teacher, have washed your feet, you ought to wash each other's feet. I have given you an example to follow. Do as I have done to you. Now that you know these things, God will bless you for doing them'" (John 13:12–15, 17).

Jesus didn't just wash the feet of the disciples who loved and respected Him. He washed Judas's feet as well. Jesus knew that Judas was dishonest (John 12:6) and that Satan had influenced his plan to betray Him (John 13:2). But Jesus loved and served him anyway, to such a degree that none of the other disciples knew he was the one He was referring to (John 13:22–25).

Jesus here and in Eph 5 is calling us to follow His example. To love and serve, even when we aren't loved or possibly hated. He wants us to give our lives for our wives even when we know she can't stand us and may never want to see us again. This is what the suffering we've talked so much about looks like. It will feel like we're dying (and at times we'll wish we could). Everything inside of us will want to quit.

This is why it took so long to get to the specifics of God's old/new method of marriage restoration. Without the biblical foundation (Eph 5) and insights from Jesus' sufferings (Isa 53), you most likely would have ignored or rejected it, telling yourself that God would never call you to go through such pain. If we hadn't looked at Jesus' imperative of loving Him more than our wives, you wouldn't be able to continue to love and serve while possibly being hated. If we hadn't covered His imperative of picking up crosses you most likely would have dropped the ones in your marriage. If we didn't expose the curse and the sin and mayhem it's going to cause in your marriage, there's every likelihood you'd still be stuck in confusion and frustration.

But, with these and the other insights presented, you now have (in Jesus' power) the ability to follow His example and give your life for your wife. My hope is that you will ask God to give you the ability to trust Him when He says, "Now that you know these things, God will bless you for doing them" (John 13:17).

My prayer is, that after reading this book, you can honestly answer with confidence (and some fear) that "yes, it is God's good plan to crush and grieve me for the sake of my marriage."

Thank you for purchasing and reading this book.

Contact Information

If you'd like to purchase more copies or possibly have me speak at your church, organization, or group (via web conferencing platforms, as I am unable to travel due to Sammy's needs) please feel free to visit hopeforhusbands.com for my contact information. Thanks again!

Bibliography

Swanson, J. *The Dictionary of Biblical Languages with Semantic Domains: Greek (New Testament)*. N.p.: Logos Research Systems, 1997. Electronic ed.

Tson, Josef. *Suffering, Martyrdom, and Rewards in Heaven*. Wheaton, IL: Romanian Missionary Society, 2007.

www.ingramcontent.com/pod-product-compliance
Lightning Source LLC
Chambersburg PA
CBHW052200090426

42741CB00010B/2348